When Behavior Makes Learning HARD

Positive Steps for Changing Student Behavior

Council for Exceptional Children
The voice and vision of special education

Barbara E. Baditoi, Ed.D.

Library of Congress Cataloging-in-Publication Data

When Behavior Makes Learning Hard
Positive Steps for Changing Student Behavior
1st printing
p. cm.
Includes bibliographical references (p.)

ISBN 0-86586-448-9 (paper)

Copyright 2010 by the Council for Exceptional Children, 1110 N. Glebe Road, Suite 300, Arlington, VA 22201

Graphic Design and Layout: Carol L. Williams

Printed in the United States of America

10 9 8 7 6 5 4 3 2 1

Dedication

With thanks to my friends, family, and colleagues,
who supported my vision
and sustained my spirit.

This book is dedicated to the committed educators who teach our children
the tools they need to change their behavior,
so education is meaningful
and learning is not hard.

Good basic
book on behavioral
management plans
and terms and
concepts
(I keep as a reference)

Table of Contents

List of Figures

About the Author

Barbara E. Baditoi, Ed.D., is a retired Director of Special Education and Student Services. Dr. Baditoi has over 29 years of building and district wide experience in public education; she was the first ED teacher hired in Fairfax County Public Schools. Over the years, she also has served as a K-12 ED/LD teacher, High School Department Chair for an ED program, Autism Resource Teacher, Behavior Specialist, and Assistant Principal. She is currently an adjunct Professor of graduate education courses at Marymount University, supervises student teachers, and is an educational consultant and author.

Dr. Baditoi earned her doctorate in education from Virginia Polytechnic Institute and State University in the area of education leadership. She earned her master's degree in the education of exceptional children from Pennsylvania State University, and her bachelor's degree in sociology from Wheaton College, Illinois. Her experience and years in education have provided her with a historical and unique perspective on engaging students with special needs.

Preface

A student who says...	Might mean...
I don't want to do this.	I can't do it.
My stomach hurts.	The bully is back.
No, I didn't finish.	I don't understand how to do it.
This math is stupid	It's too hard for me.
I didn't do my homework.	I babysat my younger sister while my mom worked.
Get out of my face.	Don't intrude on my life.
I didn't hear.	I wasn't paying attention.
You look funny.	Be my friend.
Get away from me.	My girlfriend dumped me.
I forgot my supplies.	I can't afford to buy them.
Leave me alone.	He is picking on me.
I need someone to help me.	I lack self-confidence.
You can't make me sit down.	She's bothering me and I don't know what to do.

What is the most challenging aspect of teaching students in the 21st century? Is it mastering content, applying pedagogy, learning assessment tools, analyzing individual student achievement, completing lesson plans, collaborating with colleagues, or communicating with parents? In many real-world school situations, it is not any of these, but is rather *managing student behaviors* which do not meet the norm of schoolwide and/or classroom expectations.

The ability to connect to all students in a setting that changes daily is essential in today's inclusive classroom. Schools have diverse populations, with curriculum based on legislative requirements, the age of accountability, and the demands of our global society. Behavior and academic achievement are intertwined and dependent on each other for successful progress.

Teaching academic content and managing student behavior at the same time can be tough, especially in an age of data-driven assessment and high-stakes testing. An educator's frustration in the classroom can begin with a few students demonstrating inappropriate behavior that disrupts academic routines and learning activities for all students. Teachers' goals are often thwarted by students whose behavior interferes with the educational process. Is there a way to address the behaviors that will help students achieve personal, social, and emotional independence while minimizing the impact of their behavior on staff, themselves, and others?

When Behavior Makes Learning Hard: Positive Steps for Changing Student Behavior presents a step-by-step team approach to writing behavior plans for students who exhibit challenging behavior. This workbook provides a clear and direct process school teams can follow to assess behavior and design instructional behavior plans using positive support linked to instruction in alternative strategies (sometimes referred to as *replacement behaviors*). These plans are called *instructional behavior plans* because they include instructions to assist students in recognizing their strengths and weaknesses, making changes, learning life skills, and eventually becoming responsible adults.

Ultimately, the goal of the instructional behavior plan is to assist students in changing their behavior so they can access educational opportunities and become independent learners. Changes in student behavior often necessitate modifications to the environment or instructional practices; consequently, a team effort should include a range of participants, both school- and, in some cases, home-based. Over the past 10 years, the problem-solving approach described in this workbook has been used successfully with a variety of students from pre-kindergarten to Grade 12, in both special and general education settings.

Teaching requires us to positively manage student behaviors in order to promote participation in the learning environment. When educators collaborate as they collect and analyze information, they become aware of the communicative intent of student behavior, and are able to evaluate skill deficit areas. Data is the only substantive measure of a student's true progress in both academic and behavior areas; schools and educational teams need to have a process for ongoing monitoring and modification based on the collection and assessment of data.

The approach in this workbook is based on collaboration and teaming—the concept of bringing together a team of general and special educators to analyze a behavior problem and develop positive skills-based responses. Independent of collegial input, teachers who work with students who are challenging or unresponsive operate in a vacuum in which they must facilitate learning for all students, while the behavior of one student does not improve and is also a distraction for others. The input and cooperation of like-minded educators alleviates personal stress and provides more than one set of eyes and minds to problem solve collaboratively.

The only requirement for success is the commitment of a collaborative school team dedicated to helping students open the door to improved learning experiences and social skills. In this way, educators can focus on teaching students, rather than on the behavior that makes learning hard.

Barbara E. Baditoi

Chapter 1

A Workbook Method for Assessing and Changing Student Behaviors

"COULD I USE ONE OF MY *LIFELINES*?"

Chapter 1: A Workbook Method for Assessing and Changing Student Behaviors

Teaching is exciting. Educators are dedicated and eager, knowledgeable about content and pedagogy. We step into classrooms daily, optimistic that students will respond positively to a classroom atmosphere that promotes growth and learning for all students (see Figure 1.1).

Figure 1.1. The Ideal Classroom

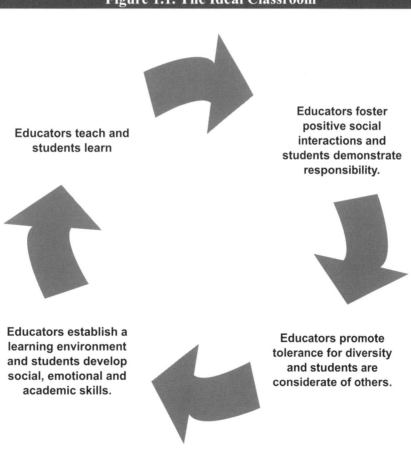

Educators teach and students learn

Educators foster positive social interactions and students demonstrate responsibility.

Educators establish a learning environment and students develop social, emotional and academic skills.

Educators promote tolerance for diversity and students are considerate of others.

... if only it were so!

Teaching and learning does not always happen reciprocally. Not all students approach learning with enthusiasm or posses the requisite readiness skills. Students who exhibit difficult and challenging behaviors perplex teachers, who wonder what triggers the behavior and how to engage and maintain student attention in the face of these behavioral challenges. Unfortunately, students with these behaviors can disrupt the class, change the classroom atmosphere, negatively impact teachers, and influence individual student outcomes. Beyond just affecting the individual student who engages in the behaviors, these students require a great deal of staff time and effort, and often test the limits of acceptable conduct in school.

Management and Support of Behavior

Alongside a full plate of curriculum content, differentiation of instruction, state-mandated testing, data-driven assessment, and ongoing progress monitoring, educators must learn and implement the difficult skill of classroom behavior management, often the most critical piece of a teacher's repertoire. Whereas skills related to instruction develop over time, the ability to implement behavior strategies is not always intuitive. A teacher facing challenges to classroom management can feel diminished and frustrated. Student disruptions impact classroom management, affecting the teacher's ability to teach and the students' opportunity to learn.

On the other hand, students need to learn to manage behavior that interferes with individual academic achievement and social and emotional development. In the same manner that teachers are used to continually adding appropriate classroom management tools to their collection of strategies, students require instruction to help them achieve life skills for the future. An educator's responsibility is not only to open up the world of knowledge, but also to offer support as students learn the rules of acceptable conduct and understand the consequences of their behavior. Part of a teacher's role is to constantly model appropriate interactions, teach appropriate skills, and support students who are attempting to change their negative behaviors.

Personal Standards and Behavior Expectations

Our diverse student population brings together a myriad of life experiences that produce the complex behaviors often seen in school. In order to positively interact with challenging students, educators need to reflect on their own values, beliefs, and preconceptions regarding instructional practices and behavior. As a teacher,

1. What are your personal preferences and limitations regarding behaviors?

2. What behaviors will you accept and tolerate, and which do you consider inappropriate and unacceptable?

3. How will you respond to students when both acceptable and unacceptable behaviors are exhibited?

4. How consistent are your responses, and what reinforcing and corrective behavior management techniques do you know or need to learn?

Educators vary in the amount and types of behaviors they expect and will tolerate in their classrooms. Based on this individual comprehensive set of rules and classroom expectations, a teacher accepts students, but not their inappropriate responses. To promote positive behavior, educators must be aware of their own individual behavioral expectations.

Expectations and tolerance levels are different for every teacher. What one teacher considers unacceptable behavior, another teacher may find acceptable. For some teachers, unacceptable student behavior may mean swearing or being disrespectful. For others, "showing good habits" and "not following directions" provide the parameters of classroom student behavior. When educators' expectations clash with students' behavior, teaching and learning are hindered and rule breaking results in consequences that impede student achievement.

Student Behavior

Student behavior is not based solely on the behavior expectations and rules identified by the teacher; it is a combination of the teacher's and the student's set of values, attitudes, and skills that translate into clear behavior expectations and performance. Just as educators enter the classroom with curriculum knowledge, research-based best practices, sound pedagogy, an educational philosophy, and personal experiences, students arrive with their own histories, relationships, academic expectations, and involvement with society and the culture of school and home. Most students adapt and thrive in the school atmosphere, but others may experience short-term situational or potentially lifelong chronic issues that affect their daily lives and hence their readiness and ability to learn.

The basic human needs of food, water, air, shelter, safety, and belonging are the building blocks for positive life experiences; a lack of these necessities and chaotic living circumstances can contribute to difficult behaviors in school. Indicators that a student may be having a personal problem outside of school include forgetting homework, refusing to follow directions, asking to go to the clinic every day, or lashing out at other students verbally or physically. Yet the underlying cause of the behavior may be the effects of environmental issues (e.g., poor nutrition and hunger, the trauma of natural disasters, war), family strife (e.g., physical, mental, and/or substance abuse; divorce; illness), economic loss (e.g., work, homelessness, poverty), or personal issues (e.g., mental health and psychological stress, chronic health problems, poor social or academic skills, lack of motivation). It is not just the simple act of the forgotten homework, walking into class late, or insubordination; when the private lives of students manifest themselves in school, accessibility to learning takes a secondary role. As educators we need to keep these issues in mind as we develop behavior support plans.

Students communicate their interests, skills, desires, needs, cultural expectations, intrinsic and extrinsic motivations, external factors, and individual personality characteristics in different ways. Before attempting to influence learning experiences and the development of acceptable behavioral skills, educators must first understand the motivation and intent of spoken and unspoken communication (see Preface). Educators have a responsibility to respond to students who, despite their best professional efforts, exhibit behavior that is not only unacceptable to their value system, but disrupts the learning process for others.

When teacher and student expectations collide, the teacher's ability to facilitate learning is hindered, and the student's access to the curriculum decreases.

Educational Milieu

The modern education environment reflects vast changes in societal structure, organizational culture, theoretical knowledge, and accountability. Legislation such as the Individuals with Disabilities Education Act (IDEA), the Elementary and Secondary Education Act (ESEA; reauthorized in 2001 as the No Child Left Behind Act, NCLB), and Section 504 of the Rehabilitation Act of 1973 require educators to recognize the relationship between student behavior and classroom learning as a shared responsibility. Teachers need to master content, rigorously assess student achievement, and at the same time address challenging behaviors. Our educational system applies the ideals of IDEA and promotes inclusion of all students; this often adds students with more complex needs to general education classroom settings. At the same time, the current response-to-intervention (RTI) approach to identifying and responding to student difficulties in learning directs that academic, social, and behavior interventions are implemented first in the general education setting.

Educators want to teach: They immerse themselves in the curriculum, differentiate instruction, assess student progress, promote enduring educational knowledge, and manage the continuous demands of the classroom. What may be more problematical is understanding and meeting the behavioral needs of students in an instructional manner that promotes personal behavior improvement, self-esteem, and growth. This requires highly skilled teachers who are confident not only with content, but with the myriad challenges of student life.

From the first passage of ESEA in the 1960s, to the Education of All Handicapped Children Act of 1975, to IDEA's "least restrictive environment" provision, federal legislation has opened the door and filled our classrooms with a variety of students with special needs. *Schoolwide positive behavior support* (PBS) is a positive, proactive process of responses by which schools determine acceptable behavior for all students. IDEA requires that IEP teams consider the use of positive behavioral interventions and supports for students whose behavior impedes their learning or the learning of other children (see 20 U.S.C. § 1414[d][3][B][i] and 34 C.F.R § 300.324[a][2][i]); a functional behavior analysis (FBA; 20 U.S.C. § 1415[k][1][F]) should be conducted when developing such interventions.

Assessing and Responding to Challenging Student Behaviors

Educators require a comprehensive approach to inclusion practices that allows students with disabilities to attend their neighborhood schools in the least restrictive environment. Behavior issues heighten the need for effective, positive, and instructional classroom management. Keeping our schools safe is imperative. Our educational mandates—both those legislated by NCLB and IDEA, and by the needs of students themselves—require us to ensure that students feel safe and secure in the school environment. The consistent and ongoing collection of data for both academic achievement and behavior necessitates a concomitant ongoing progress-monitoring approach to solving both aspects of the responsibilities of our schools.

The method of managing and improving student behaviors described in this workbook is a problem-solving approach that complements both PBS and RTI. It incorporates aspects of FBA and enables providing intensive intervention and support for students with behavior issues (i.e., RTI Tier 2 and/or Tier 3). It is a three-step process (see Figure 1.2):

1. *The behavior evaluation*. The first step in the process is to identify specifically the problem behavior and collect data; this serves as the basis for understanding the reasons for the student's behavior.

2. *The plan of action*. In developing a plan of action, the educational team outlines possible intents of the behavior; identifies the student's skill deficit areas, alternative strategies the student could use, and relevant rewards/reinforcements; and evaluates environmental/instructional changes that may be needed.

3. *The instructional behavior plan*. The completed plan should be easily applied within the school setting, rely upon previously observed student interests and skills, include strategies for implementation and follow-up data collection, and be readily available to educational team members.

This workbook describes each of these steps, and offers tips and suggestions for following the process. The appendices include sample instructional behavior plans for elementary, middle, and high school students and blank templates. The plans in Appendix A are examples of the step-by-step process; they are only examples, however. Individual student behavior evaluation and instructional behavior plans may vary in the amount of information needed in each section. The Resources listing provides suggested reading and websites for additional information.

Figure 1.2. Steps in the Process

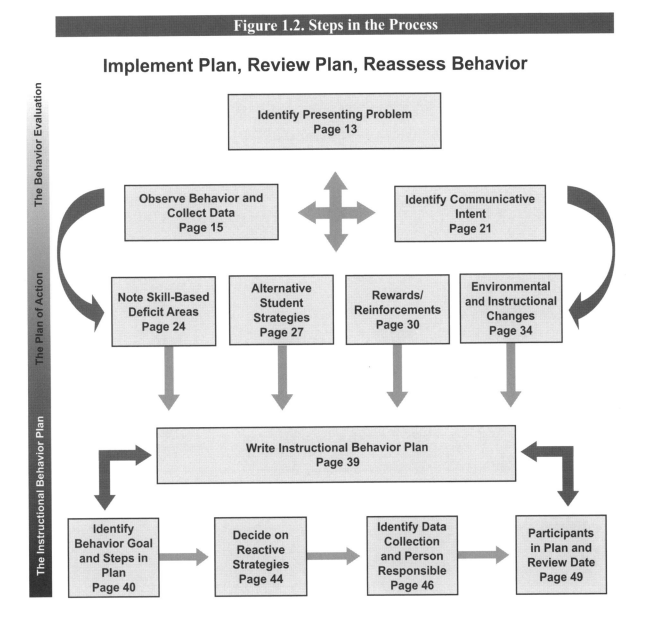

Implement Plan, Review Plan, Reassess Behavior

The Behavior Evaluation

The Plan of Action

The Instructional Behavior Plan

Identify Presenting Problem
Page 13

Observe Behavior and Collect Data
Page 15

Identify Communicative Intent
Page 21

Note Skill-Based Deficit Areas
Page 24

Alternative Student Strategies
Page 27

Rewards/ Reinforcements
Page 30

Environmental and Instructional Changes
Page 34

Write Instructional Behavior Plan
Page 39

Identify Behavior Goal and Steps in Plan
Page 40

Decide on Reactive Strategies
Page 44

Identify Data Collection and Person Responsible
Page 46

Participants in Plan and Review Date
Page 49

Following the steps, school teams can modify identified problem behaviors through positive behavior plans that instruct the student in appropriate replacement behaviors and skills. This approach is ideal for educators who are looking for a method to determine, in a straightforward manner, ways to help students change their behavior so academic progress is made, and learning is not hard.

Chapter 2

The Behavior Evaluation and Plan of Action

Behavior Evaluation and Plan of Action	
Student Name:	Date:
Grade:	School:

Section 1. Presenting Problem

Section 2. Behaviors Observed

1.

2.

3.

4.

Comments

Section 3. Data Collection of Observable Behavior

1.

2.

3.

4.

Comments

Section 4. Communicative Intent of the Behavior

1.

2.

3.

4.

Comments

Chapter 2: The Behavior Evaluation and Plan of Action

Presenting Problem

Behavior Evaluation and Plan of Action	
Student Name:	Date:
Grade:	School:
Section 1. Presenting Problem	
Section 2. Behaviors Observed	
1.	
2.	
3.	
4.	
Comments	

The *presenting problem* is a description of the problem behavior. Behaviors can range from a refusal to do academic work to not following directions or engaging in physical aggression towards peers and adults. Identifying and describing the presenting problem in a clear and objective format outlines areas of concern for school personnel. Why is the behavior an issue? Is it the severity and impact on the student, other students, the class, the teacher, and/or the learning environment? The behavior can be situational or chronic. It may be harmful to only the target student and/or harmful to others.

For example, a kindergartener who sucks her thumb presents a behavior challenge: Other children don't want to touch her hand or use material she has touched. A fourth-grade student who is off task can disrupt his class's social studies unit. Students in a middle school might be afraid of a student who hits them, although they don't respond. A senior in high school who is consistently late to class and calls out loudly to his friends when he enters distracts others; another disrupts the flow of instruction when she puts her head down and refuses to work. Table 2.1 lists the presenting problems of the students whose sample behavior evaluation and instructional behavior plans are included in Appendix A (see Appendix B for a behavior evaluation of a group of students within a class).

Table 2.1. Example of Presenting Problems

Student	Presenting Problem
Sebastian (kindergarten) Appendix A, page 61	Disrupts PE and Music class using objects inappropriately, and sometimes hurts other students
Alexis (5th grade) Appendix A, page 65	Off task during Language Arts unless working 1:1 with an adult; distracts other students
Juan (7th grade) Appendix A, page 71	Disrupts Math class
John (8th grade) Appendix A, page 77	Runs to the bus without permission; inappropriate behavior on bus (student with intellectual disabilities)
Sophia (10th grade) Appendix A, page 81	Does not complete work in more than one class; argues with teachers and is disrespectful (student with depression and learning disabilities)
Carolyn (11th grade) Appendix A, page 85	Does not follow school rules; repeated insubordination

Some student behaviors create a major disruption for the classroom or are difficult for the teacher to handle along with instruction and administrative responsibilities. The team should target the most serious of the behaviors. The team needs to decide which behavior is the most disruptive, has potentially serious consequences, or could hurt other students or staff. For example, a student who hits peers is a danger both to himself and to others; even if the student also has difficulty with work completion, safety issues come first. Once the student has achieved the goal considered to be a priority, other behavior goals can be introduced.

Behaviors Observed

Behavior Evaluation and Plan of Action	
Student Name:	Date:
Grade:	School:
Section 1. Presenting Problem	
Section 2. Behaviors Observed 1. 2. 3. 4.	
Comments	

The next step in conducting a behavior evaluation is to record the observed behaviors that support the statement of the presenting problem (see Appendix C for blank template). Listing the behaviors specifically can help the educational team in identifying underlying causes and targeting areas that need to be corrected.

During this process, it's important to be very specific about the student's problem behavior; general education and special education teachers also need to bear in mind that some behaviors might be indicative of a disability. For example, a student who sits away from her peers or turns away and refuses to participate in group activities might have an autism spectrum disorder (ASD). Students with intellectual disabilities (ID) may wait for one-to-one assistance before beginning any task. A middle-school student who complains that the work is too hard or the directions unclear might have a learning disability (LD), and a kindergartener who hides under his desk might have a mental illness or emotional disability (ED). This is by no means a comprehensive list, but rather a reminder that students with disabilities often exhibit challenging behavior or behaviors that seem not to be the norm for the student cohort.

Problem or challenging student behaviors might include:

- Being off task or disruptive during class.

- Being restless, impulsive, hyper, and disorganized.

- Not following directions, breaking rules, or being insubordinate.

- Making noises, crying, screaming, swearing, or calling out.

- Throwing a tantrum, whining, injuring self, or using vulgar gestures.

- Perseverating on an object or activity.

- Engaging in self-stimulation; damaging property.

- Poor group participation and social isolation.

- Cheating, lying, or stealing.

- Manipulating or bullying other students.

- Being rude, confrontational, defiant, and argumentative with adults.

- Leaving class without permission.

- Exhibiting physical aggression (pushing, pulling, hitting, biting, scratching, grabbing, throwing objects).

Sample Students (Appendix A)

Chapter 2

Consider Alexis, one of the students whose plans are included in Appendix A, her fifth-grade teacher found Alexis continually off task in class and a distraction to other students. He noted specifically the behaviors he observed in class: she was often out of her seat, she ignored directions, she talked to other students, and although she collected the appropriate materials on her desk, she wouldn't start work without prompting. Listing these observed behaviors lent support to the teacher's assessment of Alexis being off task. This also helped the educational team to start to target the specific behaviors that need to be changed for Alexis to progress.

Data Collection of Observable Behavior

Behavior Evaluation and Plan of Action	
Student Name:	Date:
Grade:	School:

Section 1. Presenting Problem

Section 2. Behaviors Observed

1.

2.

3.

4.

Comments

Section 3. Data Collection of Observable Behavior

1.

2.

3.

4.

Comments

Section 4. Communicative Intent of the Behavior

1.

2.

3.

4.

Comments

After the behavior has been identified, the educational team needs to collect data on the frequency, intensity, and duration of the behavior. This baseline data is used initially to answer a series of questions, but in the future the data also will help the staff with ongoing progress monitoring to determine if the plan has effected a behavioral change (see Chapter 4). Data collection should answer the following questions:

1. What is the behavior? (event recording) When does the behavior occur (time), and in what settings and situations? (location)

2. When did it first appear? How often does it appear? (interval recording and frequency)

3. How long does it last? (duration recording)

4. How severe is it? Does it pose a risk of physical injury to student or others? (topography)

5. With whom (other students, teachers, or administrators) is the behavior most likely to occur?

6. What events happen prior to the behavior (antecedent)?

7. What events happen as a result of the behavior (consequence)? Do consequences increase or decrease the behavior?

Using existing data such as behavior referrals, anecdotal records, time-out referrals, suspensions, and so on allows the team to begin assessing the behavior quickly. The team might also review academic work samples, grade reports, homework samples, and students' individual educational programs (IEPs) as part of data collection, and conduct interviews with the student and his or her family.

Sample Students (Appendix A)

Alexis's educational team needed to gather specifics on the types of off-task behavior she exhibited and the proximity or involvement (prompting) of an adult. They developed a data collection chart to track Alexis's behavior in Language Arts for one school week; the chart enabled the team to identify the duration of two specific problem behaviors and whether they occurred if an adult was nearby or did not occur at all when an adult was prompting her.

Another educational team took a similar approach: Juan's disruptive behavior in his Math class was tracked for frequency; the team also considered attendant antecedents and consequences.

Communicative Intent of the Behavior

Section 3. Data Collection of Observable Behavior

1.

2.

3.

4.

Comments

Section 4. Communicative Intent of the Behavior

1.

2.

3.

4.

Comments

The *communicative intent of the behavior* is the function of the behavior, or what the student is trying to communicate. As previously noted, students' behavior may contain a "hidden" message. In some cases, a student's inappropriate, insubordinate or oppositional behavior may signal a need for attention, assistance, or affection from an adult; a desire for peer approval or peer interaction; problems with authority; a desire for power, revenge, control, or intimidation; emotional distress (e.g., anger, fear, loneliness, guilt, anxiety, depression, hopelessness, frustration); or physical pain, fatigue, or effects from medication. Other students' noncompliance or refusal to follow instructions may be an indication of sensory sensitivity (to light, noise, sounds) or a need for sensory input; a lack of social skills or inability to read social cues; detachment and withdrawal from their environment;

a desire to protect valued items or maintain self-imposed boundaries; academic deficits; or a need for more challenging coursework and tasks. And, as mentioned previously, some of these behaviors may be indicative of underlying disabilities and disorders; see Table 2.2.

Table 2.2. Behaviors That May Indicate an Underlying Disorder or Disability

This type of behavior...	May be characteristic of a student with...					
	Autism spectrum disorders	Attention deficit hyperactivity disorders	Emotional disorders	English language learners	Intellectual & cognitive disabilities	Learning disabilities
Poor social skills	✔	✔	✔		✔	
Need for more (or less) sensory input	✔	✔				
Inappropriate emotional reaction	✔		✔			
Inability to follow instructions	✔	✔		✔	✔	✔
Inability to complete assignment	✔	✔			✔	✔
Difficulty with grade-level work				✔	✔	✔
Need for sequenced assignments and redirection	✔	✔			✔	✔
Need to move around	✔	✔				
Resistance to transitions or change in schedule	✔				✔	

Sample Students (Appendix A)

Carolyn, an 11th-grade girl, was insubordinate and argumentative with adults. She did not have difficulty with the content of her grade-level work; however, her educational team felt that the communicative intent of her behavior related to her need for peer approval and reflected a general disregard for authority and rules.

On the other hand, in the case of Sophia, a 10th-grader who frequently did not complete her work and argued with her teachers, the educational team felt the behavior might be related to her learning disability and possible depression, and that the pacing of the coursework was more than she could handle. By distilling the students' presenting problems and observed behaviors in a consistent format and collecting data, the two teams were able to develop hypotheses regarding the intent or function of each girl's behavior—on the surface similar, but with different communicative intent.

Chapter 2

Skill-Based Deficit Areas That Result in the Behavior

Behavior Evaluation and Plan of Action	Student Name:
Section 5. Skill-Based Deficit Areas That Result in the Behavior 1.. 2. 3. 4.	
Comments	
Section 6. Alternative Student Strategies Used to Achieve the Same Purpose 1. 2. 3. 4.	

Identifying *skill based deficit areas* enables the educational team to establish the student's needs, which will assist in developing an instructional behavior plan. Some students may need additional instruction, have a processing weakness, require social skill development, **may** lack motivation—or they may have an underlying disability (see Table 2.3).

Table 2.3. Skill-Based Deficit Areas

Skill-Based Deficit	Example
Students with difficulty with content may exhibit inappropriate behavior to avoid admitting their academic skill deficit.	A first-grade student hides under his desk during Language Arts.
Students with good academic skills but little motivation to perform may not turn in homework or complete class work.	A teenager rarely completes her class work in Biology.
Students with a social performance deficit may require social skills training so they can engage appropriately in social situations.	A middle-school student stands too close to her peers.
Students with autism may have difficulty asking for help appropriately	A fourth-grade boy shouts for his teacher's attention.
Students with intellectual disabilities may lack verbal communication skills.	A seventh-grade boy points, grunts, or makes noises to indicate he wants something.
Students with autism often have limited group skills.	A boy in high school withdraws and does not participate in cooperative group activities.
Students with emotional disorders may lack cooperative work or play skills.	An eight-grade girl is physically aggressive when expressing her frustration, wants and needs.
Gifted students may be bored with academic content.	A second-grade boy falls asleep in class.
Students with hearing impairments may need visual cues.	A third-grade girl does not complete work on time.
Students with learning disabilities might not complete an essay assignment.	A boy in sixth grade refuses to write an essay.

Chapter 2

Sample Students (Appendix A)

Sebastian, a kindergartener, presented problems in his PE and Music classes. His gross motor skills were greater than his ability to follow rules; he also had difficulty generalizing respecting adult authority from his classroom teacher to other adults. His educational team, by completing this section of the behavior evaluation, were able to pinpoint skills he lacked and where he required additional instruction and support.

Alexis, the fifth-grade student who was consistently off task during Language Arts, lacked independent work skills and the ability to tune out external distractors. Understanding this gave her educational team a starting point for supporting her in improving her classroom behavior and academic performance.

Alternative Student Strategies to Achieve the Same Purpose

Behavior Evaluation and Plan of Action	Student Name:
Section 5. Skill-Based Deficit Areas That Result in the Behavior	
1..	
2.	
3.	
4.	
Comments	
Section 6. Alternative Student Strategies Used to Achieve the Same Purpose	
1.	
2.	
3.	
4.	
Comments	

Chapter 2

Alternative strategies are substitute methods a student could use to achieve the same purpose currently accomplished by using inappropriate behavior. Identifying these replacement behaviors enables the educational team to assist the student in making progress toward academic, social/emotional growth, and development.

Sample Students (Appendix A)

Alexis needed to acquire alternative strategies both to help her manage writing tasks that were difficult for her and to manage the anxiety and stress she felt about her writing performance.

Juan, the seventh-grader who disrupted his Math class, needed to learn alternative strategies for asking for assistance and working independently—and for monitoring his own behavior.

Writing these strategies on their behavior evaluation forms (see Appendix A) helped their educational teams specify targeted skills to be incorporated in the students' instructional behavior plans.

Table 2.4 lists some disruptive behaviors, alternate strategies students could use to achieve the same goal, and the application of these strategies for students with disabilities.

Table 2.4. Alternative Means to the Same End: Strategies for Students

Behavior	Alternative Strategies	May be useful for students with...
Shouts for teacher's attention	Raises hand; waits to be called on	Intellectual disabilities; autism
Runs	Walks	Learning disabilities; emotional disorders; attention deficit hyperactivity disorder
Points to objects	Uses words	Intellectual disabilities
Waits for teacher to help	Asks for assistance	Learning disabilities
Rejects assistance	Accepts help when offered	Emotional disorders
Hits	Keeps hands to self	Learning disabilities; emotional disorders; attention deficit hyperactivity disorder
Teases	Speaks nicely to peers	Learning disabilities; emotional disorders
Non-completion of homework	Advocates for more time on assignments	Attention deficit hyperactivity disorder
Uses a confrontational or inappropriate tone of voice	Modulates voice	Autism; emotional disorders
Requires individual assistance	Works independently	Learning disabilities; emotional disorders; attention deficit hyperactivity disorder
Blames others	Accepts responsibility for outcomes	Emotional disorders
Bullies	Walks away and avoids criticism of others	Learning disabilities; emotional disorders; attention deficit hyperactivity disorder

Chapter 2

Possible Rewards/Reinforcements to Increase Desired Behavior

A *reward or reinforcement* is an item or activity of importance to the student that increases, decreases, or modifies the problem behavior or maintains the desired behavior. The reward/reinforcement is delivered after the student exhibits the targeted behavior.

Types of reinforcers include *primary* (material), *social* (people), or *intrinsic* (grades). The rate of reinforcement is contingent on the student's need and capacity for immediate or delayed rewards. A *token economy* is based on a symbolic representation exchangeable for a reinforcer of value to the student: it is visual, tangible, and portable (e.g., tokens, chips, points, tickets). Whereas social reinforcers appeal to students who want to spend time with friends or a favorite adult, intrinsic motivators appeal to students who respond more to personal reinforcement and pride in success.

Reinforcers need to be acceptable to both the teacher and the student (see Table 2.5); to be effective they should be desirable, immediate, and contingent on a clearly defined behavior. Students should participate in identifying desirable rewards, and/or complete inventories, motivational assessments, and reinforcement menus so they take ownership of their behavior. Teachers who use token systems should have a plan for fading the reinforcer. The goal of any behavior plan is to move from more frequent to less frequent rewards, and ultimately to self-control and internal incentives. Students are different, and their ability and motivation to internalize appropriate behavior is variable. If the plan works with frequent rewards, it should be continued at that level for a period of time. As the student exhibits behavior that approximates or achieves the targeted behavior, the frequency of rewards can be reduced.

Students may become bored with identified reinforcers after an extended period of use, so rewards often need to be reassessed. If possible and appropriate, changing the reward schedule is also the time to involve middle and high school students in reviewing the plan, discussing the behavior changes noted by staff, looking at the data, and engaging in a conversation about modifying the plan. Students of all ages may provide insight into their behavior, state whether or not the rewards are working, if they feel that the plan needs to be continued, or if the current behavior plan has achieved its goal.

Behavior Evaluation and Plan of Action	Student Name:

Section 5. Skill-Based Deficit Areas That Result in the Behavior

1..
2.
3.
4.

Comments

Section 6. Alternative Student Strategies Used to Achieve the Same Purpose

1.

2.

3.

4.

Comments

Section 7. Possible Rewards/Reinforcements to Increase Desired Behaviors

1.

2.

3.

4.

Comments

Section 8. Environmental and Instructional Changes to Modify Behaviors

1.

2.

3.

4.

Comments

Table 2.5. Acceptable Reinforcers/Rewards

For Students in Elementary School	For Students in Secondary School
Visit office or another teacher	Reading magazines
Visit to counselor	Playing video game
Help younger students	Making announcements
Tutor younger students	Structured free time
Lunch with principal or favorite teacher	Eat lunch with teacher
Homework pass	Listen to MP3 Player
Stickers	Play board or card games
Happy notes sent home	Tutor a younger student
Sit in teacher's chair or rocker	Computer time
Assist custodian or librarian	No-homework passes
Move desk to spot of own choosing	Food coupons
Structured free time	Assist with clerical work
Talk to a friend for 10 minutes	Earn bonus bucks
Drawing, puzzles	Dropping the lowest grade on a quiz or homework grade
Read a book or choose a book for the teacher to read to the class	Free pass to school event or activity
Extra recess	Opportunity to choose classroom seat
Listen to music on MP3 Player	
Assist in cleaning classroom	
Erase whiteboard	
Collect papers	
Line leader for a day	
Give message over intercom	
Get a drink of water at own choosing	
Run errands	
Earn tickets for free time	
Choice of healthy snacks (raisins, crackers, mile)	
Teach the class about a favorite subject	
Make class or school announcements	

Sample Students (Appendix A)

Sebastian, the kindergartener who disrupted his Music and PE classes, was motivated by both social and intrinsic reinforcers. His team recognized that offering him time with a special friend or admired adult, as well as special jobs and time to spend on things he enjoyed doing, would help promote his acquisition of appropriate behaviors in these classes.

Alexis, although in fifth grade, was similarly motivated; her reinforcers included time to draw with friends, a special lunch "date" with a peer and a school adult, and published works she could bring home to share with her family.

Environmental and Instructional Changes To Modify Behaviors

Behavior Evaluation and Plan of Action	Student Name:

Section 5. Skill-Based Deficit Areas That Result in the Behavior
1..
2.
3.
4.

Comments

Section 6. Alternative Student Strategies Used to Achieve the Same Purpose
1.
2.
3.
4.

Comments

Section 7. Possible Rewards/Reinforcements to Increase Desired Behaviors
1.
2.
3.
4.

Comments

Section 8. Environmental and Instructional Changes to Modify Behaviors
1.
2.
3.
4.

Comments

Classroom or school *environmental and instructional changes* (see Table 2.6) may be needed to assist the student in modifying the behavior. This is the only component of the plan of action in which school staff make changes to external stimuli.

Table 2.6. Classroom Environmental and Instructional Changes

Environmental Changes	Instructional Changes
Scheduling of activities	Using space to support instruction
Physical arrangement of the room (seating, teacher's desk, technology, proximity to door, centers, leisure area) Safe area Sit and move cushions	Differentiation of instruction: nature and variety of materials, tasks and activities; pacing of content; appeal to different modalities Varying assessment methods
Computer access	Visual displays and charts
Staffing ratio	Verbal prompts and cues
Privacy requirements (calming or cool down space/study carrels)	Social skills, self-assessment and self monitoring training
Sensory stimuli (lighting, clutter, levels of noise, temperature) Electrical outlets	Attention span of students Scheduling of routines and transitions/sensory breaks
Traffic patterns Density of students	Technology use Enriched environment
Organizational support	Additional instructional needs: before/after school activities, tutoring, mentoring

Sample Students (Appendix A)

Of our sample students, Alexis's behavior required the school to make instructional changes; Sebastian, Juan, John, and Carolyn needed environmental changes; and Sophia needed both. By completing the process of evaluating the students' behavior, the educational teams were able to then identify the students' individual needs and develop an outline of responding to those needs.

The plan of action is just that: a precise yet easy to use plan that includes guidelines for collecting information and analyzing data, and strategies and approaches for students to assist them in changing problem behaviors. This part of the process leads to development of the individual student's instructional behavior plan.

Chapter 3

The Instructional Behavior Plan

It was not until they entered the principal's office that the Keppelmans realized the severity of Ryan's discipline problem.

Instructional Behavior Plan	
Student Name:	Date:
Grade:	School:

Meeting Attendees

Behavior Plan and Goal:

1.
2.
3.

Reactive Strategies

1.
2.
3.
4.

Data Collection Tool/Person(s) Responsible

1.
2.
3.
4.
5.

Participants in Plan

1.	4.
2.	5.
3.	6.

Date to review plan (within two weeks of implementation):

Chapter 3: The Instructional Behavior Plan

The purpose of the instructional behavior plan is to teach students alternative strategies for coping and new ways to communicate their intent: it is *instructional* because when the plan is successfully implemented, the student learns new skills. The instructional behavior plan provides a process by which the educational team applies what it learned in conducting the behavior evaluation and plan of action, and should respond to the essential questions considered in the first two stages:

1. What is the underlying communicative intent of the student's behavior?

2. What are the student's skill based deficit areas?

3. What alternative strategies does the student need to learn?

4. What reinforcers would be successful to enhance the student's positive behavior?

5. What environmental and instructional changes does the school need to make?

The instructional behavior plan specifically describes the goal as well as the strategies and approaches to be used to achieve it; the plan should incorporate the student's reinforcers (see page 30), reactive strategies to respond to noncompliant behavior, and a process for data collection to assess the effectiveness of the plan. It also identifies participants in the plan and a date to review the plan, to ensure ongoing progress monitoring. A blank template of the instructional behavior plan is included in Appendix C.

Behavior Plan and Goal

Instructional Behavior Plan	
Student Name:	Date:
Grade:	School:
Meeting Attendees	
Behavior Plan and Goal: 1. 2. 3.	
Reactive Strategies 1. 2. ?	

The overall behavior goal articulates the aim of the instructional behavior plan, and provides a quantitative measure to assess student progress. Its articulation of the behavior goal is, again, *instructional*: the student is taught a replacement behavior and therefore does not need to use inappropriate behavior to communicate intent. This section of the template (see Appendix C) lists the steps for implementation and monitoring student progress toward the goal and the reinforcer/reward. The plan should note under what conditions the student will complete the behavior: independently, with assistance, with minimal direction or with intermittent verbal reminders.

Figures 3.1 and 3.2 on page 42, provide additional examples of this section of the instructional behavior plan, for Miranda, a fifth-grade student, and Antoine, a seventh-grade student.

Sample Students (Appendix A)

For Sebastian, the overall goal was to improve his behavior in PE and Music class. His articulated goal was that he would "listen to directions 9 out of 10 times and appropriately use PE equipment 90% of the time." To track this quantitatively, his PE and Music teachers would award him checkmarks for both aspects; for each class twice a week, he could earn two checkmarks. The plan incorporated both an immediate and a delayed reinforcement: Receiving two checkmarks in either class enabled him to help the teachers put the instruments and equipment away at the end of class. If he earned a total of four checkmarks from each class in a week, Sebastian would get to shoot hoops with the PE teacher.

Chapter 3

Figure 3.1 Miranda's Behavior Plan and Goal

Instructional Behavior Plan	
Student Name: *Miranda*	Date: *October 15, 2009*
Grade: *5*	School: *Walnut Elementary*

Meeting Attendees

Language Arts and Math teachers, administrators, school counselor, case manager

Behavior Plan and Goal: *Miranda will raise her hand when asking for assistance 75% of the time in Language Arts and Math.*

1. *Miranda will receive a checkmark each time she raises her hand instead of calling out for help during Language Arts and Math.*
2. *Miranda will add up her checkmarks after Language Arts and Math (each check equals 10 points).*
3. *Miranda will post her final tally at the end of the day on a chart kept in her desk.*
4. *On Monday, Wednesday and Friday, Miranda will use her cumulative points to buy computer time during lunch. (Points are given each day, but used 3 days/week).*

Figure 3.2 Antoine's Behavior Plan and Goal

Instructional Behavior Plan	
Student Name: *Antoine*	Date: *February 10, 2010*
Grade: *7*	School: *Forest Middle School*

Meeting Attendees

Math and PE teachers, administrator, school counselor

Behavior Plan and Goal: *Antoine will complete his in-class work in Math class and write down his homework 80% of the time.*

1. *Mark receives two checks from his teacher at the end of Math 8 class: one for completed work, and one for writing down his homework (on a block schedule, a total of six checks are possible for the week).*
2. *At the end of the week, Mark independently counts his checks and uses them for extra time in the gym to shoot hoops with the PE teacher. He must have (three checks) to spend 10 minutes in the gym at the end of the day.*
3. *After two weeks, he will need to earn five checks for 10 minutes.*

Reactive Strategies

Instructional Behavior Plan	
Student Name:	Date:
Grade:	School:
Meeting Attendees	
Behavior Plan and Goal: 1. 2. 3.	
Reactive Strategies 1. 2. 3. 4.	
Data Collection Tool/Person(s) Responsible	

Reactive strategies (Table 3.1) are used when a consequence for behavior is imposed inside or outside the classroom. Reactive strategies in the classroom are often behavior management strategies. Because they are disciplinary in nature and negative in implementation, reactive strategies used outside the classroom should only be used when a student breaks school rules, inflicts harm to self or others, or violates the local code of conduct. Federal legislation now requires more accountability with regard to inappropriate school behavior that results in an out-of school-consequence, so the use of these strategies should be carefully considered.

Sample Students (Appendix A)

The behavior goal for John (a student with intellectual disabilities), was for him to exhibit appropriate behavior on the bus. Reactive strategies that the educational team planned, to be implemented when he did not exhibit the desired behavior, included escorting him to the bus (implemented in school) and loss of TV time at home (implemented outside of school).

Table 3.1. Reactive Strategies

Implemented in the classroom	Implemented outside the classroom
Planned ignoring	Loss of building activities (lunch with peers, assemblies, field trips)
Redirection	
Corrective procedures	Time out
Removal of preferred objects	Phone call to parents
Proactively involving parents	Parent conference
Loss of activities, points, privileges	Detention (lunch or after school)
Reinforcement not earned	In-school suspension
	Out-of-school suspension

Data Collection for Instructional Behavior Plan/Person(s)

Instructional Behavior Plan	
Student Name:	Date:
Grade:	School:
Meeting Attendees	
Behavior Plan and Goal: 1. 2. 3.	
Reactive Strategies 1. 2. 3. 4.	
Data Collection Tool/Person(s) Responsible 1. 2. 3. 4. 5.	
Participants in Plan	

Data collection tools enable the educational team to monitor the plan's implementation. The data collection tool may need to be developed specifically to track the student's targeted behavior. Appendix A includes data collection charts developed specifically for each student to collect the data needed to assess whether our sample students were meeting their goals.

Chapter 3

Sample Students (Appendix A)

Sebastian's PE and Music data collection charts were developed to record the checkmarks he could receive twice a week for following directions and using instruments appropriately.

Alexis's data chart enabled an observer to record her on-task or off-task behavior in 10-minute increments throughout her Language Arts class.

Juan's self-monitoring behavior chart and Sophia's chart focused on appropriate classroom behavior.

John's bus behavior chart is an example of a pictograph chart for prereaders, students with intellectual disabilities, or struggling readers.

Appendix B includes a data collection chart for a classwide instructional behavior plan. This portion of the instructional behavior plan also identifies the person responsible for collecting the data. Generally, it should be a participant who is already involved with the student, such as a teacher, a specialist, school counselor, or support staff, and someone who will easily and quickly have access to the data.

Some of the data required to monitor the success of a student's instructional behavior plan is already collected as part of the school day (e.g., discipline referrals, visits to the clinic, classroom behavior management program records). If the plan requires too much time spent in record keeping, it will not be followed. When writing the plan, the team should look at methods of data collection that are relatively easy, accessible, and appropriate; reinforcements should be easily managed and delivered within the context of the school day and teacher responsibilities (unless the parent is involved with reinforcers delivered at home). Using simplified data collection tools streamlines the process and assures compliance with the plan.

This is also why the team approach is preferred: The teacher gives the team feedback on what has or has not worked within the classroom, which parts of the plan are unreasonable due to classroom limitations, and which behavior strategies and reinforcement the student can engage in without disrupting classroom instruction. A variety of staff members sharing in the plan implementation also provides assistance for the classroom teacher.

Chapter 3

Participants in the Plan/Review Date

Instructional Behavior Plan	
Student Name:	Date:
Grade:	School:
Meeting Attendees	
Behavior Plan and Goal: 1. 2. 3. 4.	
Reactive Strategies 1. 2. 3. 4.	
Data Collection/Person(s) Responsible 1. 2. 3. 4.	
Participants in Plan 1. 2. 3. 4.	
Date to review plan (within two weeks of implementation):	

The *participants in the plan* are adults participating in the behavior plan who either have a relationship with the student, or can contribute to the analysis of the behavior. Only those people who are a critical part of the ongoing progress monitoring of the student need to attend the initial writing of the behavior plan. If the plan has a home component, a parent or guardian should be part of the process.

Participation by School Staff Members

Staff members who participate in student instructional behavior plans may include, but are not limited to:

- General education and special education teachers

- School counselor

- Department chairs/team leaders

- Specialists (e.g., speech and language clinician, occupational or physical therapist), itinerant teachers, coaches

- Administrator

- School social workers and school psychologists

- Parents or guardians

- Instructional assistants or paraprofessionals

- Attendance officer

- Mentors and volunteers

- Clerical, custodians, secretaries, food service workers

Staff members who participate in writing the plan will have a stake in its success. Whether or not they are part of the plan's implementation, their involvement will add support and acknowledge the seriousness of the problem. Such an approach assumes that all team members want to help improve student behavior and that they may participate in monitoring or implementing the plan. If staff seems reluctant to participate, the administrator may have to remind them of their responsibilities to all students—including those with challenging behaviors.

Student Participation

High school students should take part in developing the instructional behavior plan; not only is their input crucial, but is mandatory to ensure that they will "buy in" to the plan. Middle school students also could take part in giving input and writing the instructional behavior plan. Elementary school students, as mentioned in Chapter 3, can be involved in helping to identify reinforcers and, in some cases, self-monitoring their behavior. (However, the first-stage analysis of the behavior is more the purview of the educational team.)

Generally, students are capable of self-monitoring their behavior when they understand the nature of their actions and the reasons for staff concern. They are able to have meaningful discussions about learning alternative strategies, and may welcome an opportunity to become part of the overall plan. The more ownership the student has, the more progress will be achieved.

Self-monitoring techniques are useful, life-long skills. Helping students to stop and think about their behavior and then implement self-monitoring strategies that have been modeled, taught and practiced, are important lessons that are critical in the real world of work and study.

Elementary students, especially in the primary grades, may only understand that they have trouble sitting still or keeping their hands to themselves, and that they receive a reward for following directions, staying in their seat, and keeping their hands to themselves. However, they also learn that they have the power to influence their decision-making and behavior-changing skills, by making positive or negative choices. They may not be capable of self-monitoring their behavior but they are aware of the behavior goals the adults consider important. Upper elementary students can often monitor themselves during the instructional behavior plan (see Alexis's plan in Appendix A for an example of a self-monitoring approach for an elementary school student).

Plan Implementation and Review

A sufficient amount of time should be given to implementing the plan. It is not unusual that an increase in disruptive behavior occurs before the plan begins to work. A student can manipulate a behavior plan so success is not achieved, and the behavior may get worse before it gets better. However, when the student realizes that the team will be consistent in following the plan, and when the rewards become a greater reinforcement than the desire to engage in inappropriate behavior, the disruptive behavior should lessen. A behavior plan is not static: adjustments and modifications need to be applied to ensure continued success.

If the plan has been consistently implemented but the behavior remains seriously challenging and the team is concerned about whether or not student needs are being met, another meeting should be called—even if it's before the scheduled review date. Perhaps there are situations occurring outside school that were not present when the first plan was written, or the dynamics within the classroom have changed. The team may decide to move to another level of intervention that includes a different approach, such as a referral to an outside agency, or implementing behavior consequences that are administrative in nature.

When the team meets to review the plan, the data can be analyzed to determine if the targeted behavior is changing. The behavior plan should be implemented for a specified length of time, usually about 2 weeks, and then evaluated for effectiveness. Has the behavior improved across a variety of settings and activities or is it still exhibited in certain areas (e.g., have visits to the clinic declined? has the student's work completion increased)? If the plan is not working, it must be modified. Behavior plans are not static and are only effective if they increase the desired behavior, decrease the inappropriate behavior, and instruct the student in using alternative or replacement strategies to achieve the desired behavior.

Chapter 4

Frequently Asked Questions (FAQs)

Chapter 4: Frequently Asked Questions (FAQs)

How can an educational staff create simple but effective plans?

➢ Use the templates in Appendix C to develop simple, workable and effective instructional behavior plans.

➢ Have all information available during the planning stage to facilitate the process.

➢ Use data collection tools to ensure that plans are monitored for effectiveness.

➢ Designate a team member to facilitate the planning meeting, take notes, fill out the template, and ensure that all team members receive a copy. (This could be the case manager for a special education student, or, for general education students, the school counselor or administrator.)

➢ Focus on one behavior that needs to be changed.

➢ Set a time to reassess the plan.

How does a team decide which behavior to focus on when there is more than one disruptive behavior?

Some students exhibit behaviors that create a major disruption for the classroom, or that are difficult for the teacher to handle along with instructional and administrative responsibilities. The team needs to decide which behavior is the most disruptive, has potentially serious consequences, or could hurt other students or staff—and target that behavior first.

Chapter 4

The plan looks overwhelming. How do I follow it and teach at the same time?

Clearly, the role of the classroom teacher is a complex one that requires fast thinking in many different areas. A behavior plan that is too ambitious or difficult will not be followed. The plan needs to incorporate data-keeping measures and reinforcements that can be easily managed and delivered within the context of the school day. The team approach also supports the classroom teacher in implementing the behavior plan.

How do we find the time to do data collection?

Data collection and monitoring progress is an ongoing process, and often incorporates information that is already collected during the school day. The team should consider data tools that are easily used, accessible, and appropriate to streamline the process and ensure compliance.

Do all students with behavior issues require behavior plans?

Not all students with challenging behaviors require behavior plans: some students respond to less structured interventions such as a discussion with the counselor or a meeting with the administrator. The decision to write a behavior plan is individual and based on the needs and responses of the student.

What if the behavior becomes more disruptive?

It is not unusual that an increase in disruptive behavior occurs before the plan begins to work. However, if the team is consistent in following the plan, the rewards become more reinforcing than the motivation for the bad behavior.

When should a behavior plan shift from more frequent to less frequent rewards?

The goal of any behavior plan is to move from more frequent to less frequent rewards, and ultimately to student self-control and internal incentives. The frequency of rewards should be reduced as the student exhibits behavior that approximates or achieves the targeted behavior.

How do we involve all staff members in monitoring the plan?

Staff members who participate in writing the plan will have a stake in seeing it succeed. Sometimes, however, administrators need to remind staff of their responsibilities to all students —including those with challenging behaviors.

Should we involve students in developing and implementing the plan? How?

The involvement of middle and high school students is crucial to ensuring their "buy in" to the plan. Even younger students can help identify appropriate reinforcers. Both elementary and secondary students also can learn self-monitoring and self-asssessment skills by participating in monitoring their progress with the plan.

What are some ideas for involving parents in the plan?

Parents should be informed that school staff is concerned about their child's behavior, and that, as part of the team approach, parental input is welcomed. Parents can participate in writing and monitoring the plan or as part of the positive reinforcement system used to increase the desired behavior. The more parents are involved, the greater the benefit to the students, and the stronger the possibility that the plan will be successful. Parental support is always a powerful tool to use in changing student behavior.

Who is ultimately responsible for overseeing a student's instructional behavior plan?

This is a team decision. If it is a special education student, in all likelihood the case manager will be ultimately responsible. However, if assistance is available from a behavior specialist, team leader, or administrator, the responsibility can be shared. For example, the classroom teacher gives stars for a targeted behavior, the counselor provides the reward, the principal compliments the student on improved behavior, and the parent supplies an additional reward outside school. The culture of the school dictates how student behaviors are viewed and accepted, the level of teamwork, who will manage the plan and who will collect the data.

Chapter 4

How do we explain the plan reinforcers to other students?

With the practice of full inclusion and the diversity of students in our schools, many students are accustomed to the concept of their peers being treated differently, but equitably. When questioned by students about a particular student's plan, a fairly common response is "Everybody learns differently, and I am helping Brian learn" or "Brian and I are working on some things together." Confidentiality is always a key component of any behavior plan; reinforcers and data collection should be as unobtrusive as possible. Having adults other than the classroom teacher participate in delivering rewards could solve the problem of explaining the reinforcers to classmates. Sometimes an entire class of students is working together on a behavior plan (see Appendix B).

Appendix A

Sample Student Behavior Evaluation and Plan of Actions, Instructional Behavior Plans, and Data Collection Tools

Sebastian

Behavior Evaluation and Plan of Action	
Student Name: *Sebastian*	Date: *September 30, 2009*
Grade: *Kindergarten*	School: *Roosevelt Elementary School*

Section 1. Presenting Problem

In Phys Ed and Music, Sebastian uses classroom objects inappropriately (balls in PE and instruments in Music), and sometimes hurts other students.

Section 2. Behaviors Observed

1. *Throws balls at other students in PE. Uses equipment inappropriately.*

2. *Runs around gym when asked to sit; does not follow adult directions.*

3. *Kicks balls at wall, knocks over cones.*

4. *In Music, tries to hit others with his musical instrument.*

Comments

Sebastian exhibits inappropriate behavior when participating in less structured activities (PE and Music). He has a high amount of energy.

Section 3. Data Collection of Observable Behavior

1. *Physical Education and Music teacher tallied number of times materials and equipment were used inappropriately, and talked to Sebastian about his behavior.*

2. *PE and Music teachers kept a phone log of number of times parents were called.*

3. *Referrals to administrator.*

4. *Number of students sent to the clinic as a result of Sebastian's behavior.*

Comments

As the year progresses Sebastian's behavior in Music and PE has escalated. Concurrently, his classroom teacher notes he has also used classroom tools (crayons, pencils) inappropriately

Section 4. Communicative Intent of the Behavior

1. *Sebastian struggles with basic kindergarten skills, does not complete his work, and is frustrated by the time he goes to PE and Music.*

2. *He likes to play with his peers, but does not understand PE rules.*

3. *Sebastian is seeking adult and peer attention.*

4. *He is upset about his classroom performance and kicking balls and hurting other children is an outlet for his anger.*

Comments

Sebastian has good gross motor skills and moves around the gym quickly. He may like the adult attention he obtains when he uses equipment inappropriately.

Behavior Evaluation and Plan of Action	Student Name: *Sebastian*

Section 5. Skill-Based Deficit Areas That Result in the Behavior

1. *Sebastian does not comprehend that rules must be followed in locations other than his classroom.*
2. *Sebastian's gross motor skills are better than his ability to participate appropriately in the activities.*
3. *He does not generalize adult authority from his classroom teacher to other adults.*
4. *Sebastian does not have the words to reflect his need for physical activity.*

Comments

Sebastian may not understand that aggression is not a game and peers can be hurt.

Section 6. Alternative Student Strategies Used to Achieve the Same Purpose

1. *Sebastian could review PE expectations using laminated visual cue cards before each activity.*

2. *He could use the PE equipment and musical instruments in appropriate ways.*

3. *Sebastian could work with the school counselor to learn new vocabulary to use when he is not in control of his behavior.*

4. *He could interact with peers in a more appropriate manner, including asking them to play.*

Comments

Sebastian often exhibits the same behaviors in recess, but seems to calm down after five minute time outs on the blacktop. He is more easily redirected in Music than PE.

Section 7. Possible Rewards/Reinforcements to Increase Desired Behaviors

1. *Earn time alone with PE teacher and a friend in a sports activity.*

2. *Earn the responsibility of becoming ball and equipment class assistant after PE.*

3. *Earn 15 minutes of free time with peers in monitored PE activities.*

4. *Earn 10 minutes 3 times/week in music room to bang on drums.*

Comments

Sebastian says he likes to shoot hoops and bang on drums.

Section 8. Environmental and Instructional Changes to Modify Behaviors

1. *Proximity seating near teachers with verbal and visual cueing when directions are given.*

2. *Counselor teaches Sebastian importance of rules, and provides opportunities for him to practice.*

3. *Use soft balls to modify impact of throwing; give instruments to student only when needed.*

4. *Modify instruction by giving Sebastian an individual warm-up exercise in PE.*

Comments

The PE teacher is impressed with Sebastian's physical abilities

Instructional Behavior Plan	
Student Name: *Sebastian*	Date: *October 21, 2009*
Grade: *Kindergarten*	School: *Roosevelt Elementary School*

Meeting Attendees

Classroom, PE, and Music teachers; school counselor; administrator; parent (by speaker phone)

Behavior Plan and Goal: *Sebastian will listen to directions 9 out of 10 times and appropriately use PE equipment and Music instruments 90% of the time.*

1. With the school counselor, Sebastian will create a social story about appropriate PE and Music behavior. He will review it everyday before going to PE or Music.

2. Sebastian will receive two checks in PE and two checks in Music for (a) following directions, and (b) using equipment correctly. (He has both PE and Music twice each week).

3. If Sebastian earns two checks by the end of PE, he will assist the teacher in picking up the equipment.

4. If Sebastian earns two checks by the end of Music, he will assist the teacher in putting away the instruments.

5. At the end of the week, if he has four checks each from PE and Music, he will spend eight minutes shooting hoops with the PE teacher, during designated time.

Reactive Strategies

1. During PE, 5-minute time out seated in a designated gym space for not following directions.

2. Referral to administrator if Sebastian throws a ball or other equipment and hits a peer; removed from class for 10 minutes (or for an appropriate time period).

3. Parent is phoned if Sebastian hurts other students during PE or music by inappropriately using equipment or instruments. Parent is asked to process the incident with Sebastian and emphasize the importance of rules and safety.

Data Collection/Person(s) Responsible

1. Number of checks earned in PE and Music using Data Collection Charts (PE and Music teachers).

2. Monitor number of times Sebastian throws items and hits other children (PE and Music teachers).

3. Monitor reports from the clinic of students hurt as a result of Sebastian's behavior (Clinic Room Assistant).

4. Monitor amount of times spent shooting hoops with PE teacher (Classroom and PE Teacher).

Participants in Plan

1. Physical Education teacher	*4. Administrator*
2. Kindergarten teacher	*5. School counselor*
3. Music teacher	*6. Parent*

Date to review plan (within two weeks of implementation): *November 4, 2009*

Sebastian's Instructional Behavior Plan Data Collection Charts

Physical Education Data Collection				
Week of		**Teacher s Signature**		
Followed directions			Day 1	Day 2
Used PE equipment appropriately			Day 1	Day 2

Music Data Collection				
Week of		**Teacher s Signature**		
Followed directions			Day 1	Day 2
Used Music instruments appropriately			Day 1	Day 2

Alexis

Behavior Evaluation and Plan of Action	
Student Name: *Alexis*	Date: *October 1, 2009*
Grade: *5*	School: *Hemlock Elementary School*

Section 1. Presenting Problem

Alexis engages in off-task behavior in Language Arts unless she is working 1:1 with an adult. She distracts other students in the room. She requires writing skills for the 5th grade state exams.

Section 2. Behaviors Observed

1. *Out of seat during Language Arts.*

2. *Ignores adult when reminded to sit down and complete work..*

3. *Talks to friends or draws instead of following directions, especially during writing.*

4. *Gathers materials on desk but then ignores them.*

Comments

Alexis's inability to begin and remain on task during writing activities creates classroom disruption. She interacts with her peers when they are trying to work.

Section 3. Data Collection of Observable Behavior

1. *Off task approximately 50% of time without adult intervention (see data collection chart).*

2. *On task when adult sitting with her or in close proximity to her desk (see data collection chart).*

3. *Requires at least 5 adult verbal prompts to begin work in Language Arts, especially in writing (see data collection).*

4. *Non-completion of work as documented in grade book.*

Comments

Alexis likes hands-on activities. Her lack of independent work skills are more noticeable during writing. She says that writing "hurts her hands."

Section 4. Communicative Intent of the Behavior

1. *External distractions interfere with her ability to focus.*

2. *She is anxious about her writing, and does not know how to begin the task.*

3. *She wants to be liked by her friends and seeks peer approval.*

4. *Alexis is discouraged about her writing, especially when she watches other students complete essays.*

Comments

Alexis is easily distracted, and may not be able to control her off-task behavior. An Occupational Therapy screening noted that her fine motor skills are age appropriate.

Page 1 of 2

Appendix A

Behavior Evaluation and Plan of Action	Student Name: *Alexis*

Section 5. Skill-Based Deficit Areas That Result in the Behavior

1. *Lack of independent work skills.*

2. *Inability to control anxiety regarding writing performance.*

3. *Cannot ignore external distractors and lacks self-calming techniques.*

4. *Does not understand pre-writing skills.*

Comments

Alexis sometimes asks her friends if they "would rather write or draw."

Section 6. Alternative Student Strategies to Achieve the Same Purpose

1. *Increase independent work skills for writing tasks.*

2. *Use alternative methods for writing if available (computer, tape recorder).*

3. *Learn pre-writing strategies (graphic organizers, mapping).*

4. *Acquire stress reducing and self-calming techniques.*

Comments

A reduction in Alexis' anxiety and distractibility may improve her writing skills.

Section 7. Possible Rewards/Reinforcements to Increase Desired Behaviors

1. *Pair drawing with writing tasks.*

2. *Lunch with a peer and school counselor or adult mentor.*

3. *Reading and writing with a younger student.*

4. *Publish writing and drawing for school publications or home use.*

Comments

Alexis is sociable and liked by peers and younger students. She completed an interest and motivation inventory.

Section 8. Environmental and Instructional Changes to Modify Behaviors

1. *Calming tools that provide motivation to write, such as "special" pens (roller balls, gel, colors).*

2. *Preparation of behavior chart for daily use.*

3. *Use of headphones during writing tasks.*

4. *Availability of alternative methods for writing (access to writing lab or writing desk).*

5. *Resource assistance from Reading Teacher or other staff member.*

Comments

Alternative methods should be faded once Alexis has learned pre-writing skills and can begin the assignment.

Alexis's Behavior Evaluation and Action Plan Data Collection Chart

Independent Work Behavior Data Collection										
Student Name *Alexis*				**Week of** *September 28☐October 2, 2009*						
Course/Class				**Case Manager** *Jennifer Stanton*						
Language Arts				**Observer** *Margie Temple (Instructional Assistant)*						

Date	Time		Out of seat	Not following verbal or written directions	Talking	# of adult verbal prompts	Completed work?		Time on task	
	Begin	End					Yes	No	W/adult assistance	Adult in proximity
9/28	*9:55*	*10:00*							*5 min*	
9/29	*10:00*	*10:50*	|||			||				*10 min*

Comments

Instructional Behavior Plan	
Student Name: *Alexis*	Date: *October 8, 2009*
Grade: *5*	School: *Hemlock Elementary School*

Meeting Attendees

Language Arts teacher, school counselor, reading teacher, resource teacher, parent

Behavior Plan and Goal: *Independent work 50% of time in Language Arts*

1. *Alexis will complete 45 minutes of independent work during a 90-minute Language Arts period.*

2. *The Language Arts teacher awards Alexis a checkmark for every 10 minutes she exhibits on-task behavior. A total of 9 checkmarks is possible each day; Alexis's goal is 5 per day or more.*

3. *Alexis will total her checks each day and enter on spreadsheet.*

4. *To receive a reward at the end of the week, Alexis must earn 25 checks or more for the week.*

5. *School rewards include lunch time with a friend and the counselor, or time with her first-grade reading buddy.*

6. *Home rewards include extra TV time if homework and in-class work completed.*

Reactive Strategies

1. *Alexis will receive an "X" for every 10 minutes she exhibits off-task behavior.*

2. *If not enough checks are earned, she does not earn a special lunch with a friend and the counselor, or time with her first-grade buddy.*

3. *Language Arts teacher monitors checkmarks, and if Alexis receives fewer than 22 checks/week, parent is called and asked to make sure Alexis completes homework before watching TV.*

Data Collection/Person(s) Responsible

1. *Time On-Task Data Collection Chart; monitor number of checkmarks earned during 2-week period (Language Arts teacher)*

2. *Independent completion of pre-writing task (classroom teacher).*

3. *Number of times earned visit with peer and first grade buddy (first grade teacher).*

4. *Amount of times Alexis earns lunch with the school counselor and a friend (Counselor).*

Participants in Plan

1. *Language Arts teacher*	4. *Reading teacher*
2. *Student*	5. *School counselor*
3. *Parent*	6. *Teacher of first-grade reading buddy*

Date to review plan (within two weeks of implementation): *October 22, 2009*

Alexis's Instructional Behavior Plan Data Collection Chart

On-Task Work Behavior Data Collection					
Student Name: *Alexis*		**Begin Date**			
Course/Class: *Grade 5 / Language Arts*		**End Date**			
= On-task behavior = Off-task behavior					
Week 1					
Time Period	**Monday**	**Tuesday**	**Wednesday**	**Thursday**	**Friday**
10:00-10:10					
10:10-10:20					
10:20-10:30					
10:30-10:40					
10:40-10:50					
10:50-11:00					
11:00-11:10					
11:10-11:20					
11:20-11:30					
Total					
Week 2					
10:00-10:10					
10:10-10:20					
10:20-10:30					
10:30-10:40					
10:40-10:50					
10:50-11:00					
11:00-11:10					
11:10-11:20					
11:20-11:30					
Total					
Total, both weeks					
Total for 2-week period:		**Teacher signature:**			
25 checks = lunch with friend and counselor or extra time with reading buddy					

Juan

Behavior Evaluation and Plan of Action	
Student Name: *Juan*	Date: *January 5, 2010*
Grade: *7*	School: *Coleridge Middle School*

Section 1. Presenting Problem

Juan consistently disrupts his Math class with inappropriate behaviors. Instructional time is impacted. Class meets at 10:15 each day for 45 minutes.

Section 2. Behaviors Observed

1. *Calls out, shouts obscenities during instruction.*

2. *Gets out of seat, moves around room.*

3. *Refuses to follow teacher's directions.*

4. *Draws on paper when math instructions are given.*

Comments

Approximately 50% of math time, Juan is off task and disruptive during math. His peers find it difficult to concentrate. Removing him from class has minimal impact.

Section 3. Data Collection of Observable Behavior

1. *Instances of inappropriate behavior (see Data Collection Chart; recorded by Math Teacher).*

2. *Number of visits to the school counselor to discuss inappropriate behavior in math.*

3. *Number of referrals to the time-out room for disrespect (shouting obscenities).*

4. *Number of times referred to after-school detention by administrator.*

Comments

Behaviors are escalating. Referrals to administrator or 30-minute monitored time-outs have had minimal impact.

Section 4. Communicative Intent of the Behavior

1. *Juan is frustrated with math and does not understand the content.*

2. *He wants to be noticed by his peers..*

3. *He is seeking adult attention.*

4. *He can't concentrate during math because he is hungry and needs a snack.*

Comments

Juan remains focused for short periods of time when he is 1:1 with an adult. He sometimes asks how long until lunch and complains of being hungry.

Page 1 of 2

Behavior Evaluation and Plan of Action	Student Name: *Juan*

Section 5. Skill-Based Deficit Areas That Result in the Behavior

1. *Lack of appropriate communication skills to verbalize needs.*

2. *Needs alternative ways to gain adult assistance.*

3. *Slow processing of math content.*

4. *Juan has math anxiety regarding state-required math exams.*

Comments

Juan hates math and says it does not make sense. He has failed state-mandated math tests.

Section 6. Alternative Student Strategies to Achieve the Same Purpose

1. *Raise hand to receive teacher assistance.*

2. *Complete math problems independently.*

3. *Meet with teacher during lunch for extra assistance.*

4. *Meet with counselor to learn how to modify disruptive behavior through self-monitoring strategies.*

Comments

Juan talks about his inappropriate behavior with the school counselor, but does not understand why he does it or how to control his behavior.

Section 7. Possible Rewards/Reinforcements to Increase Desired Behaviors

1. *Through phone calls, administrator communicates positive and appropriate behavior to parent.*

2. *Reading time in room at end of math.*

3. *Become library assistant at end of day twice a week.*

4. *Collect books from classrooms and take to library (book collector)..*

Comments

Juan is motivated by books about fantasy worlds. He has a good relationship with the librarian. Juan will complete an interest and reinforcement inventory.

Section 8. Environmental and Instructional Changes to Modify Behaviors

1. *Proximity seating near teacher*

2. *Pair with math buddy.*

3. *Change math to first block/period of day.*

4. *Allow a small snack (brought from home) before math*

Comments

Math is midway through the morning and before lunch.

Juan's Behavior Evaluation and Action Plan Data Collection Chart

Date:		
Antecedent *What occurs right before the behavior?*	**Behavior** (Note time of occurrence)	**Consequence** *What occurs after the behavior?*
	Out of Seat	
	Calls Out	
	Moves Around Room	
	Shouts Obscenities	
	Does Not Follow Directions	

Instructional Behavior Plan	
Student Name: *Juan*	Date: *January 20, 2010*
Grade: *7*	School: *Coleridge Middle School*

Meeting Attendees

Math teacher, school counselor, math specialist, administrator, librarian

Behavior Plan and Goal: *Juan will decrease inappropriate behavior in math by 25% in 3 weeks.*

1. Juan will self-monitor his behavior in math by giving himself checkmarks every 15 minutes for appropriate behavior (staying in his seat, not calling out, not shouting obscenities, and following teacher directions).

2. Juan and his math teacher sign the check sheet.

3. At the end of the day, Juan takes his check sheet to the librarian.

4. If he has earned 50% of his checks (during a 45-minute block he will need 7 out of a possible 15 checkmarks), he assists the librarian at the end of the day.

Reactive Strategies

1. Sent to time-out room after two disruptive behaviors (out of seat and moving around room, calling out, shouting obscenities, not following teacher direction).

2. Administrator talks to Juan about his behavior after first time out.

3. Administrator calls parent after second time in one week.

4. Time out is limited to 20 minutes.

5. Counselor explores with Juan his behavior choices, outcomes and options.

Data Collection/Person(s) Responsible

1. Daily behavior charts (Math teacher).

2. Monitor number of time-out referrals (time-out monitor).

3. Monitor number of administrative interventions/referrals (Administrator)

4. Monitor checks earned and number of times Juan assists the librarian (Librarian).

Participants in Plan

1. *Math teacher*	5. *School counselor*
2. *Librarian*	6. *Student*
3. *Parent*	7. *Time-out monitor*
4. *Administrator*	

Date to review plan (within two weeks of implementation): *February 3, 2010*

Juan's Daily Behavior Monitoring Chart

Time Period	During this time period, I...	During this time period, I...
9:30–9:45	Used appropriate words Listened to the teacher Stayed in my seat Followed directions Completed my work	Used inappropriate words Talked back to the teacher Got out of my seat Ignored class rules Did not complete my work
9:45–10:00	Used appropriate words Listened to the teacher Stayed in my seat Followed directions Completed my work	Used inappropriate words Talked back to the teacher Got out of my seat Ignored class rules Did not complete my work
10:00–10:15	Used appropriate words Listened to the teacher Stayed in my seat Followed directions Completed my work	Used inappropriate words Talked back to the teacher Got out of my seat Ignored class rules Did not complete my work
TOTAL		
Student signature:		**Teacher signature:**

John

Behavior Evaluation and Plan of Action	
Student Name: *John*	Date: *February 10, 2010*
Grade: *8*	School: *Polk Secondary School*

Section 1. Presenting Problem

John has intellectual disabilities. He runs to the bus without permission every day after school. On the bus, he often engages in unsafe or inappropriate behavior.

Section 2. Behaviors Observed

1. *Running to and between buses.*

2. *Trying to kiss girls or touching other students.*

3. *Getting out of his seat on the bus.*

4. *Not following directions to walk to his bus.*

Comments

John presents both safety issues and behavior issues relating to riding the bus.

Section 3. Data Collection of Observable Behavior

1. *Number of bus referrals sent from bus driver to teacher.*

2. *Number of bus incident reports completed by bus driver and given to administrator.*

3. *Bus supervisor keeps phone log of number of phone calls to parent.*

4. *Number of complaints from students and parents.*

Comments

Written bus incident reports have been given to the administrator. Verbal reports are usually for lesser infractions.

Section 4. Communicative Intent of the Behavior

1. *Wants attention from bus driver and other students.*

2. *Wants to go home and is afraid of missing his bus.*

3. *Is interested in girls.*

4. *He wants friends but does not know how to make them.*

5. *He wants to be first on the bus.*

Comments

John does well in school until it is almost time to go home.

Page 1 of 2

Behavior Evaluation and Plan of Action	Student Name: *John*

Section 5. Skill-Based Deficit Areas That Result in the Behavior

1. *Does not understand social skills or personal space.*

2. *Does not understand bus rules and expectations.*

3. *Has difficulty standing in line and waiting for bus.*

4. *Does not comprehend safety issue.*

Comments

Safety issues and bus rules have been discussed and practiced with John numerous times..

Section 6. Alternative Student Strategies Used to Achieve the Same Purpose

1. *Practice self-regulation strategies while walking to bus.*

2. *Meet a bus buddy in school and walk to bus.*

3. *Be escorted by paraprofessionals to bus before regular dismissal.*

4. *Learn appropriate bus social skills.*

Comments

John's IEP goals include independent daily living skills, including transportation.

Section 7. Possible Rewards/Reinforcements to Increase Desired Behaviors

1. *Sit with a peer on bus 3 times a week.*

2. *Choose his favorite bus seat once a quarter.*

3. *Stars/checkmarks on behavior management chart from bus driver.*

4. *Carry favorite age-appropriate object on bus.*

5. *Additional video game time at home.*

Comments

Parent is concerned about John's bus behavior and has agreed to reward him at home with additional video game time.

Section 8. Environmental and Instructional Changes to Modify Behaviors

1. *Change paraprofessional schedule so John can be escorted to bus.*

2. *Adapt class schedule so John can leave his last class early.*

3. *Provide a behavior checklist for bus driver to complete and give to staff.*

4. *Seat John directly behind the bus driver and have attendant on bus.*

Comments

John needs to learn and practice new skills

Page 2 of 2

Instructional Behavior Plan	
Student Name: *John*	Date: *February 10, 2010*
Grade: *8*	School: *Polk Secondary School*

Meeting Attendees

Special education teacher, bus driver, parent, paraprofessional, administrator

---

Behavior Plan and Goal: *John will exhibit appropriate behavior on the bus 90% of the time.*

1. *At the end of the day, John is escorted to the bus by a paraprofessional and receives one star for walking.*

2. *John receives up to 2 stars from bus driver for sitting in seat, keeping hands to self, and exhibiting appropriate bus behavior.*

3. *Parent receives chart and awards John extra TV time (10 additional minutes for each star).*

4. *Parent e-mails special education teacher with number of stars earned each day.*

Reactive Strategies

1. *If John runs or bolts to bus, he is escorted to the office by staff member*

2. *Parent is called and staff escorts John back to the bus.*

3. *John loses TV time that evening at home.*

4. *Bus incident reports are submitted to administrator, who speaks to John.*

Data Collection/Person(s) Responsible

1. *Bus Stars chart (bus driver/parent)*

2. *Bus incident reports (bus driver, special ed teacher, administrator)*

3. *Weekly tally of bus stars (parent, special ed teacher)*

Participants in Plan

1. *Special education teacher*	4. *Paraprofessional*
2. *Bus driver*	5. *Administrator*
3. *Parent*	

Date to review plan (within two weeks of implementation): *February 24, 2010*

John's Bus Stars Chart

Date:		Bus Driver's Initials
SITS IN SEAT	KEEPS HANDS TO SELF	WALKS TO BUS
AM	AM	PM Only
PM	PM	

Sophia

Behavior Evaluation and Plan of Action	
Student Name: *Sophia*	Date: *January 29, 2010*
Grade: *10*	School: *Chester Arthur High School*

Section 1. Presenting Problem

Sophia does not complete work in English; in Civics, she is in danger of failing for the year. She argues with her co-teachers and calls them names. Mother informed staff that Sophia takes medication for depression. She was found eligible for LD services in 8th grade.

Section 2. Behaviors Observed

1. *Work refusal, puts head down on desk.*

2. *Comes to class unprepared and without homework.*

3. *Argues with teachers and is disrespectful; does not follow directions.*

4. *Poor attention to task; does not complete work in class; failing grades.*

Comments

Sophia has only completed 50% of her English assignments. She is doing slightly better in Civics. Interim grades were D in Civics and F in English.

Section 3. Data Collection of Observable Behavior

1. *Grades*	3. *Number of times suspended for disrespectful behavior towards adults*
2. *Number of referrals to administrators*	4. *Anecdotal teacher records*
3. *Number of phone calls to mother; parent conferences*	5. *Records review*

Comments

Sophia is more belligerent after the weekends. Class meets every other day from 12:30 to 1:15 PM..

Section 4. Communicative Intent of the Behavior

1. *Sophia is embarrassed by her lack of reading skills.*

2. *Co-taught classes are stressful and she may find the pace of the instruction too fast.*

3. *Mother has been diagnosed with cancer, and Sophia watches her younger siblings after school. She sees her father on weekends.*

4. *Internal issues (depression) are affecting her ability to complete work.*

Comments

Sophia was in self-contained LD classes last year and her grades were better. The late lunch time may affect her performance and attitude.

Behavior Evaluation and Plan of Action	Student Name: *Sophia*

Section 5. Skill-Based Deficit Areas That Result in the Behavior

1. *Poor comprehension skills, especially in content areas.*

2. *Lacks independent work and organizational skills.*

3. *Cannot focus in class because of anxiety about her family and/or depression.*

4. *Does not understand how to ask for assistance from adults in appropriate manner.*

5. *Lacks motivation and has poor coping skills.*

Comments

Sophia claims grades don't matter, but she often asks if she is passing. Math is her strength.

Section 6. Alternative Student Strategies to Achieve the Same Purpose

1. *Use pre-reading strategies to approach content areas.*

2. *Learn techniques to interact with adults appropriately.*

3. *Check in with school counselor during lunch or before school to verify that assignments are in planner and material is organized.*

4. *Use a cool down or break pass to visit school counselor to discuss coping strategies.*

Comments

Sophia is working on pragmatic language skills to use when she is frustrated.

Section 7. Possible Rewards/Reinforcements to Increase Desired Behaviors

1. *"No homework" passes.*

2. *Passing grades.*

3. *Tutor in math lab, or work with a peer needing math assistance.*

4. *Complete an interest and/or reinforcement inventory to determine motivators.*

Comments

Sophia has a positive relationship with her math teacher.

Section 8. Environmental and Instructional Changes to Modify Behaviors

1. *Change to self-contained classes for English and/or Civics after talking to Sophia and her mother.*

2. *Change time of day of classes so English and Civics are before lunch.*

3. *Increase Speech and Language time via IEP addendum.*

4. *Discuss medication issues with mother, and contact social worker for referrals to outside supports.*

Comments

Sophia told her school counselor she does not like her new medication. With her agreement, the counselor shared this information with the mother.

Page 2 of 2

Instructional Behavior Plan	
Student Name: *Sophia*	Date: *January 29, 2010*
Grade: *10*	School: *Chester Arthur High School*

Meeting Attendees

Case manager, school counselor, Civics and English teachers, parent, parent liaison, speech and language therapist

Behavior Plan and Goal: *Sophia will stay on task 50% of the time, complete class work for Civics and English, and be respectful towards adults.*

1. Sophia can receive 2 checkmarks per class (English and Civics) for using appropriate language, and 2 for work completion.

2. Teachers enter the checkmarks on a chart in Sophia's assignment book and initial.

3. Two checkmarks per day allows Sophia to assist the Math teacher in the Math Lab after school on A days.

Reactive Strategies

1. Disrespectful or argumentative behavior referred to administrator

2. Administrator may assign in-school or out-of-school suspension(s).

3. Administrator will call parent for disrespectful or argumentative behavior, followed by phone call from case manager or parent liaison.

4. School counselor provides parent liaison with behavior plan progress. Parent liaison contacts mother and gives verbal feedback on implementation of the plan.

Data Collection/Person(s) Responsible

1. Daily behavior plan charts in assignment book (Civics and English classroom teachers).

2. Administrative referrals for disrespectful or argumentative behavior (administrator)

3. Passing grades (Civics and English classroom teachers, special education case manager, school counselor)

4. Number of times Sophia assists in Math lab each week

Participants in Plan

1. *Math and Civics teachers*	4. *Student*
2. *Special Education case manager*	5. *Administrator*
3. *Parent*	6. *School counselor*

Date to review plan (within two weeks of implementation): *February 12, 2010*

Sophia's Daily Behavior Plan Monitoring Chart

DATE: _____	DATE: _____
English	English
Civics	Civics
Respectful Behavior [ ]	**Respectful Behavior** [ ]
Work Completion [ ]	**Work Completion** [ ]
Achieved Goal: Yes_____ No _____	**Achieved Goal: Yes_____ No _____**

Carolyn

Behavior Evaluation and Plan of Action	
Student Name: *Carolyn*	Date: *November 5, 2010*
Grade: *11*	School: *Main Street High School*

Section 1. Presenting Problem

Carolyn is a bright student whose main interests are her peers, especially her boyfriend. She does not like following school rules and has been suspended for insubordination.

Section 2. Behaviors Observed

1. *Argumentative and insubordinate with adults.*

2. *Refuses to follow school rules.*

3. *Arrives late to class especially on Monday.*

4. *Leaves class without permission to see her friends at prearranged times.*

Comments

When Carolyn chooses to perform academically, she does well and can earn passing grades. She is intolerant of peers not in her social group.

Section 3. Data Collection of Observable Behavior

1. *Number of tardies per quarter*	3. *Grades*
2. *Number of behavior referrals for arguing with adults*	4. *Anecdotal teacher records*
3. *Number of in-school suspensions for insubordination or tardiness*	

Comments

Since late October, Carolyn has escalated her behavior.

Section 4. Communicative Intent of the Behavior

1. *Carolyn believes rules are meant to be broken; she claims only ⬚losers⬚ follow rules.*

2. *She does not respect authority and appears to want to maintain her ⬚tough⬚ persona.*

3. *Her boyfriend and friends are more important to her than school rules.*

4. *Weekends are stressful for Carolyn because both parents want to spend time with her.*

Comments

Logical consequences have no impact on her behavior, and she can usually manage passing grades. Her mother is absent from the home and her father works long hours.

Page 1 of 2

Behavior Evaluation and Plan of Action	Student Name: *Carolyn*

Section 5. Skill-Based Deficit Areas That Result in the Behavior

1. *Lack of ability or lack of interest and motivation to regulate behavior and follow rules.*

2. *Poor adult relationships.*

3. *Lack of long-term goals: primary reinforcers are short-term relationships.*

4. *Does not care about the relationship between her behavior and consequences, especially since she ultimately passes most classes.*

Comments

Carolyn has a history of poor peer and adult relationships. She does well in Art.

Section 6. Alternative Student Strategies to Achieve the Same Purpose

1. *Follow school rules and regulations..*

2. *Prioritize needs versus wants and short-term objectives versus long-term goals.*

3. *Develop respect for adults and their roles.*

4. *Learn anger management techniques and improve social skills.*

Comments

Carolyn has no post-high school plans. She states it does not matter what she does, but has talked to her school counselor about going to college to get away from home.

Section 7. Possible Rewards/Reinforcements to Increase Desired Behaviors

1. *Time with an adult mentor.*

2. *Time each week to use Art Lab.*

3. *Improvement in grades.*

4. *Weekly discussion with counselor regarding academic goals and career planning, self-regulation strategies and positive choices*

Comments

Midway through her junior year, the pressure of post high school planning may affect her performance.

Section 8. Environmental and Instructional Changes to Modify Behaviors

1. *Change her schedule so she is not with her boyfriend in any classes.*

2. *For first period or block, shadow Carolyn to class so she is on time.*

3. *Informally enlist her friends support to lessen tardiness.*

4. *Have Carolyn check in with counselor on Monday morning.*

Comments

Carolyn does not want her schedule changed. Carolyn will complete an interest inventory.

Instructional Behavior Plan	
Student Name: *Carolyn*	Date: *November 12, 2009*
Grade: *11*	School: *Main Street High School*

Meeting Attendees

School counselor, administrator, teachers, student

Behavior Plan and Goal: *Carolyn will attend class on time each period and exhibit appropriate behavior in class 90% of the time.*

1. *Written contract for Carolyn completed with her input.*

2. *Enlist Carolyn's "buy in" through use of interest inventory and goal setting.*

3. *Target getting to class on time, staying in class, and treating adults with respect.*

4. *Carolyn receives time in the Art Lab (based on interest inventory) for weekly fulfillment of the contract.*

Reactive Strategies

1. *After-school detention for non-completion of work.*

2. *In-school suspension for insubordination.*

3. *Teachers call parent after 2 tardies in any class*

4. *Impact on grades for unexcused tardies; 9 unexcused tardies equal failure for the quarter*

Data Collection/Person(s) Responsible

1. *Signed contract and check-ins (School Counselor).*

2. *Monitor behavior referrals for insubordination (Administrator).*

3. *Monitor tardies (School records).*

4. *Amount of time spent in Art Lab (monitored by Art teacher).*

Participants in Plan

1. *School counselor*	4. *Administrator*
2. *Teachers*	
3. *Student*	

Date to review plan (within two weeks of implementation): *November 30, 2009*

Contract Between Carolyn and Main Street High School

I, **Carolyn**, want to obtain passing grades so I have a chance of attending college. I understand that my behavior often interferes with my school work.

With my counselor, Ms. Smith, I have set the following personal goals:

1. Arrive to class on time.

2. Stay in class.

3. Complete my work.

4. Interact respectfully with adults.

My long-term goal is _____. To help me reach my goals, it would be helpful if my teachers would:

1. Remind me of my long-term goals.

2. Help me stay on track with my class work.

In addition to receiving better grades, I would like to meet with Ms. Smith twice a week for ⬚check in⬚ and twice a month to review my goals. I would also like to spend extra time in the Art Lab. I understand that I must maintain a B average in order to complete this contract.

If I do not fulfill the terms of this contract, I realize there may be more severe consequences such as suspension from school and failing grades.

I am willing to work to meet the goals of this contract and I appreciate the assistance of my teachers.

Signed (Student): _____ Date: _____

Signed (School Counselor): _____ Date: _____

Signed:(Teacher): _____ Date: _____

Signed: (Teacher): _____ Date: _____

Appendix B

Sample Class Behavior Evaluation and Action Plan, Instructional Behavior Plan, and Data Collection Tool

Class Sample

Behavior Evaluation and Plan of Action	
Student Name: *LD Algebra I Class*	Date: *September 30, 2009*
Grade: *9*	School: *Sequoia High School*

Section 1. Presenting Problem

Inappropriate classroom behavior of four 9th grade LD students in a self-contained Algebra I class disrupts the classroom and makes learning difficult.

Section 2. Behaviors Observed

1. *Teasing, joking, name calling, whistling, primarily directed at each other.*

2. *Invading the space of other students.*

3. *Disrespectful toward adults.*

4. *Refusing to work.*

Comments

The four 9th grade students feed off each other when engaging in inappropriate behavior.

Section 3. Data Collection of Observable Behavior

1. *Number of behavior referrals to department chair and administrator.*

2. *In-school suspension for disrespectful behavior towards adults.*

3. *Number of phone calls, e-mails to parents, and requests for parent conferences.*

4. *ABC (antecedent, behavior, consequence) observations completed by paraprofessional.*

Comments

Data of disruptive behavior has been documented by the paraprofessional assigned to this class. Some students are in danger of failing the course.

Section 4. Communicative Intent of the Behavior

1. *Low academic skills in content area; individual academic achievement is not a goal.*

2. *Desire to establish dominance among peers..*

3. *Lack of behavior expectations from parents; peer approval is more important.*

4. *After-school responsibilities impact ability of students to do homework.*

Comments

Students state that parents work two jobs and are rarely home and that their peer group is important to them.

Page 1 of 2

Behavior Evaluation and Plan of Action	Student Name: *LD Algebra I Class*

Section 5. Skill-Based Deficit Areas That Result in the Behavior

1. *Poor academic skills, especially in math. Two of the students are also English language learners.*

2. *Inability to begin and complete tasks.*

3. *Unable or unwilling to accept responsibility for behavior especially in front of peers.*

4. *Lack of appropriate group and classroom social skills.*

Comments

Some of the students are friends outside of school. Peer relations are important.

Section 6. Alternative Student Strategies to Achieve the Same Purpose

1. *Exhibit appropriate behavior with peers.*

2. *Comply with adult requests.*

3. *Participate in group goal setting targeting appropriate social interactions.*

4. *Complete assigned work.*

Comments

Algebra I is a required course for a high school diploma.

Section 7. Possible Rewards/Reinforcements to Increase Desired Behaviors

1. *Eating snacks in class.*

2. *Earn structured free time to play games or talk at the end of class.*

3. *Earn homework or break passes, or free passes to attend positive school events.*

4. *Pizza party twice a month*

Comments

Check with administration regarding use of food as reinforcer due to food allergies.

Section 8. Environmental and Instructional Changes to Modify Behaviors

1. *Weekly 20-minute short-term social skills group led by school psychologist, social worker, or counselor.*

②. *Change seating daily or weekly to separate students.*

3. *Place paraprofessional in middle of group.*

Comments

Short-term counseling group will impact math time.

Instructional Behavior Plan	
Student Name: *LD Algebra I Class*	Date: *September 30, 2009*
Grade: *9*	School: *Sequoia High School*

Meeting Attendees

Algebra teacher, LD Chair, administrator, Math specialist, social worker/school psychologist/school counselor, special education case manager

Behavior Plan and Goal: *All students will exhibit on task behavior 80% of time..*

1. *On a rotational basis, students take data for 10 minutes every day. Each student begins with 100 points each day. Points are awarded for appropriate behavior and subtracted for inappropriate behavior.*

2. *On Friday points are tallied, discussed in class, and spent on computer or game time. Goal is 480 points per student per week.*

3. *Twice a month, class participates in pizza party.*

Reactive Strategies

1. *Administrative behavior referrals for disrespectful or argumentative behavior.*

2. *Following school policy, calls to parents for excessive referrals*

3. *After school detention or mandatory study hall*

4. *Grades reflect lack of completed work*

Data Collection/Person(s) Responsible

1. *Behavior data collection chart (students, Algebra teacher).*

2. *Administrative referrals and consequences (Administrator).*

3. *Points at end of week tallied by students. Teacher retains point sheet (students and Algebra teacher).*

4. *Calculation of number of agreed-upon activities earned (Algebra teacher, LD Chair).*

5. *Number of social skills groups completed (School psychologist, social worker, or school counselor).*

Participants in Plan

1. *Algebra teacher*	4. *Administrator*
2. *Students*	5. *Social worker, school psychologist, or counselor (for short-term social skills group)*

Date to review plan (within two weeks of implementation): *October 14, 2009*

LD Algebra Class Behavior Plan Data Collection Chart

Daily Behavior Monitoring Chart					Observer:				
Positive Behavior Observed					**Negative Behavior Observed**				
Behavior	Student A	Student B	Student C	Student D	Behavior	Student A	Student B	Student C	Student D
Polite to peers					Impolite to Peers:				
					Teasing, taunting				
					Name calling				
					Nasty remarks				
Polite to adults					Impolite to Adults:				
					Disrespectful /defiant				
					Not following directions				
Verbally appropriate					Inappropriate verbally:				
					Making jokes				
					Making noises, burping				
					Rattling paper				
					Whistling				
Physically appropriate					Inappropriate physically: Pushing				
					Hitting				
					Throwing small objects				
					Invading others' space				
Classwork on-task					Off-task: Refusing to work				
					Not participating in discussion				
					Not answering questions				
Accepted responsibility for actions					Not accepting responsibility for actions				
Total checkmarks					**Total checkmarks**				

Total for each student: Beginning 100 points + points for positive behavior - points for negative behavior TOTAL FOR DAY	**Student A**	**Student B**	**Student C**	**Student D**

Appendix C

Blank Templates: Behavior Evaluation and Plan of Action and Individual Behavior Plan

Behavior Evaluation and Plan of Action	
Student Name:	Date:
Grade:	School:

Section 1. Presenting Problem

Section 2. Behaviors Observed

1.

2.

3.

4.

Comments

Section 3. Data Collection of Observable Behavior

1.

2.

3.

4.

Comments

Section 4. Communicative Intent of the Behavior

1.

2.

3.

4.

Comments

Page 1 of 2

Behavior Evaluation and Plan of Action	Student Name:

Section 5. Skill-Based Deficit Areas That Result in the Behavior

1.

2.

3.

4.

Comments

Section 6. Alternative Student Strategies to Achieve the Same Purpose

1.

2.

3.

4.

Comments

Section 7. Possible Rewards/Reinforcements to Increase Desired Behaviors

1.

2.

3.

4.

Comments

Section 8. Environmental and Instructional Changes to Modify Behaviors

1.

2.

3.

4.

Comments

Instructional Behavior Plan	
Student Name:	Date:
Grade:	School:

Meeting Attendees

Behavior Plan and Goal:

1.

2.

3.

4.

Reactive Strategies

1.

2.

3.

4.

Data Collection/Person(s) Responsible

1.

2.

3.

4.

Participants in Plan

1.

2.

3.

4.

Date to review plan (within two weeks of implementation):

Resources

Atkins, M., Cullinan, D., Epstein, M., Kutash, K. & Weaver, R. (2008). *Reducing behavior problems in the elementary school classroom* (NCEE 2008-012). Washington, DC: U.S. Department of Education National Center for Education Evaluation and Regional Assistance, Institute of Education Sciences. Retrieved from http://ies.ed.gov/ncee/wwc/pdf/practiceguides/behavior_pg_092308.pdf

Bateman, B. D., & Golly, A. (2003). *Why Johnny doesn't behave: Twenty tips and measurable BIPs*. Verona, WI: Attainment.

CanTeach! (n.d.) *A list of reward ideas*. Retrieved from www.canteach.ca/elementary/classman2.html

Fairbanks, S., Simonsen, B., & and Sugai, G. (2008). Classwide secondary and tertiary tier practices and systems. *TEACHING Exceptional Children, 40*(6), 44–52.

Gable, R. A., Butler, C. J., Walker-Bolton, I., Tonelson, S. W., Quinn M. M., & Fox, J. L. (2003). Safe and effective schooling for all students: Putting into practice the disciplinary provisions of the 1997 IDEA. *Preventing School Failure, 47*, 74–77.

Gable, R. A., Hendrickson, J. M., & Smith, C. (1999). Changing discipline policies and practices: Finding a place for functional behavioral assessment in schools. *Preventing School Failure, 43*, 167–170.

Greene, R. (2008). Kids do well if they can. *Phi Delta Kappan, 90*, 161–167.

Heering, P.W., & Wilder, D. A. (2006). The use of dependent group contingencies to increase on-task behavior in two general education classrooms. *Education & Treatment of Children, 29*, 459–468.

Jones, M. (2006). Teaching self-determination: Empowered teachers, empowered students. *TEACHING Exceptional Children, 39*(1), 12–17.

Kaff, M. S., Zabel, R. H., & Millham, M. (2007). Revisiting cost-benefit relationships of behavior management strategies: What special educators say about usefulness, intensity, and effectiveness. *Preventing School Failure, 51*, 35–46.

Lane, K. L., Wehby, J. H., Robertson, E. J., & Rogers, L. N. (2007). How do different types of high school students respond to schoolwide positive behavior support programs? Characteristics and responsiveness of teacher-identified students. *Journal of Emotional and Behavioral Disorders, 15*, 3–21.

Lebrun, M. *Mini-functional behavior assessment—The fast food model to behavior assessment*. Retrieved from http://www.cec.sped.org/AM/Template.cfm?Section=Home&CONTENTID=8207&TEMPLATE=/CM/ContentDisplay.cfm

Mendler, A. N. (1992). *What do I do when...? How to achieve discipline with dignity in the classroom*. Bloomington, IL: National Educational Service.

Payton, J., Weissberg, R. P., Durlak, J. A., Dymnicki, A. B., Taylor, R. D., Schellinger, K. B., & Pachan, M. (2008) *The positive impact of social and emotional learning for kindergarten to eighth-grade students: Findings from three scientific reviews*. Chicago, IL: Collaborative for Academic, Social and Emotional Learning.

Rock, M. L. (2005). Use of strategic self-monitoring to enhance academic engagement, productivity, and accuracy of students with and without exceptionalities. *Journal of Positive Behavior Interventions, 7,* 3–17.

Rockwell, S., & Guetzloe, E. (1996). Group development for students with emotional/behavioral disorders. *TEACHING Exceptional Children, 29*(1), 38–43.

Ruef, M. B., Higgins, C., Glaeser, B. J., & Patnode, M. (1998). Positive behavioral support: Strategies for teachers. *Intervention in School and Clinic, 34,* 21–31.

Salend, S. J., & Sylvestre, S. (2005). *Understanding and addressing oppositional and defiant children's behaviors. TEACHING Exceptional Children, 37*(6), 32–39.

Simonsen, B., Sugai, G., & Negron, M. (2008). Schoolwide positive behavior supports: Primary systems and practices. *TEACHING Exceptional Children, 40*(6), 32–40.

Smith, J. O. (1995). *Behavior management: Getting to the bottom of social skills deficits.* Retrieved from http://www.ldonline.org/article/6165

Sprague, J., Cook, C. R., Wright, D. B., & Sadler, C. (2008). *RTI and behavior: A guide to integrating behavioral and academic supports.* Horsham, PA: LRP.

Sugai, G., & Horner, R. (1999). Discipline and behavioral support: Practices, pitfalls, and promises. *Effective School Practices, 17*(4), 10–22.

Sugai, G., & Horner, R. (2001, June). *School climate and discipline: Going to scale.* Paper presented at "Partners Make a Great IDEA: A National Summit on the Shared Implementation of the Individuals with Disabilities Education Act," Washington, DC.

Swaggart, B. L. (1998). Implementing a cognitive behavior management program. *Intervention in School and Clinic, 33,* 235–238.

U.S. Department of Education Office of Special Education Programs. *Technical assistance center on positive behavioral interventions & supports.* http://www.pbis.org

Virginia Department of Education. (2006). *Functional behavioral assessment, behavior intervention plans, and positive intervention and supports: An essential part of effective schoolwide discipline in Virginia* (2nd ed.). Richmond, VA: Author. Retrieved from http://www.doe.virginia.gov/support/student_conduct/functional_behavioral_assessment.pdf

Wilkinson, L. A. (2008). Self-management for children with high-functioning autism spectrum disorders. *Intervention in School and Clinic, 43,* 150–157.